EAST RIDING
OF YORKSHIRE COUNCIL

Schools Library Service

PROJECT
2021

CELEBRATIONS
Around the World

by Wil Mara

raintree

a Capstone company — publishers for children

Raintree is an imprint of Capstone Global Library Limited, a company incorporated in England and Wales having its registered office at 264 Banbury Road, Oxford, OX2 7DY – Registered company number: 6695582

www.raintree.co.uk
myorders@raintree.co.uk

Edited by Gena Chester
Designed by Julie Peters
Original illustrations © Capstone Global Library Limited 2021
Picture research by Jo Miller
Production by Spencer Rosio
Originated by Capstone Global Library Ltd
Printed and bound in India

978 1 3982 0262 7 (hardback)
978 1 3982 0261 0 (paperback)

British Library Cataloguing in Publication Data
A full catalogue record for this book is available from the British Library.

Acknowledgements
We would like to thank the following for permission to reproduce photographs: Alamy: Christian Mueringer, 7; Getty Images: John S Lander/Contributor, 23; iStockphoto: SeanShot, 6, shapecharge, 5, tovfia, 8; Newscom: Xinhua News Agency/Shao Haijun, 26; Shutterstock: Asianet-Pakistan, 11, Auribe, Cover, blueeyes, 9, DreamSlamStudio, 21, GTS Productions, 24, hbpro, 17, JG ARIF WIBOWO, 27, Jim Barber, 16, Kobby Dagan, 22, Sheila Fitzgerald, 20, Snehal Jeevan Pailkar, 12, Stephen Barnes, 25, StockImageFactory.com, 13, 28, View Apart, 4, Yeongsik Im, 15, zhao jiankang, 1, 19. Design elements: Capstone; Shutterstock: Stawek (map), VLADGRIN

CONTENTS

Words in **bold** are in the glossary.

LET'S CELEBRATE!

What do you think of when you hear the word *celebration*? Do you think of good food? Spending time with family and friends? These are great ways to **celebrate**!

Some celebrations have to do with religion. Others help us remember important days in history. There are many different **customs** around the world. Just like you, people celebrate in special ways!

RELIGIOUS HOLIDAYS

A religion is a set of beliefs people follow. Many celebrations mark an important event in a religion.

Christians look forward to Christmas. It remembers the birth of Jesus. Many celebrate on 25 December. Families go to church. They give each other gifts.

A family sets up a Nativity scene.

A Christmas tree in Germany

Some people in Italy set up Nativity scenes. These show baby Jesus and his parents. In many places, Christmas trees are brought into homes. People cover them in **decorations** and lights.

Jewish people mark the new year with Rosh Hashanah. In Israel, it is usually celebrated in September for two days. Jewish people get together to pray. A ram's horn is blown. It reminds people to think about mistakes they have made. Then they think about how they can become better.

The ram's horn is called a *shofar*.

Apples with honey are eaten during Rosh Hashanah.

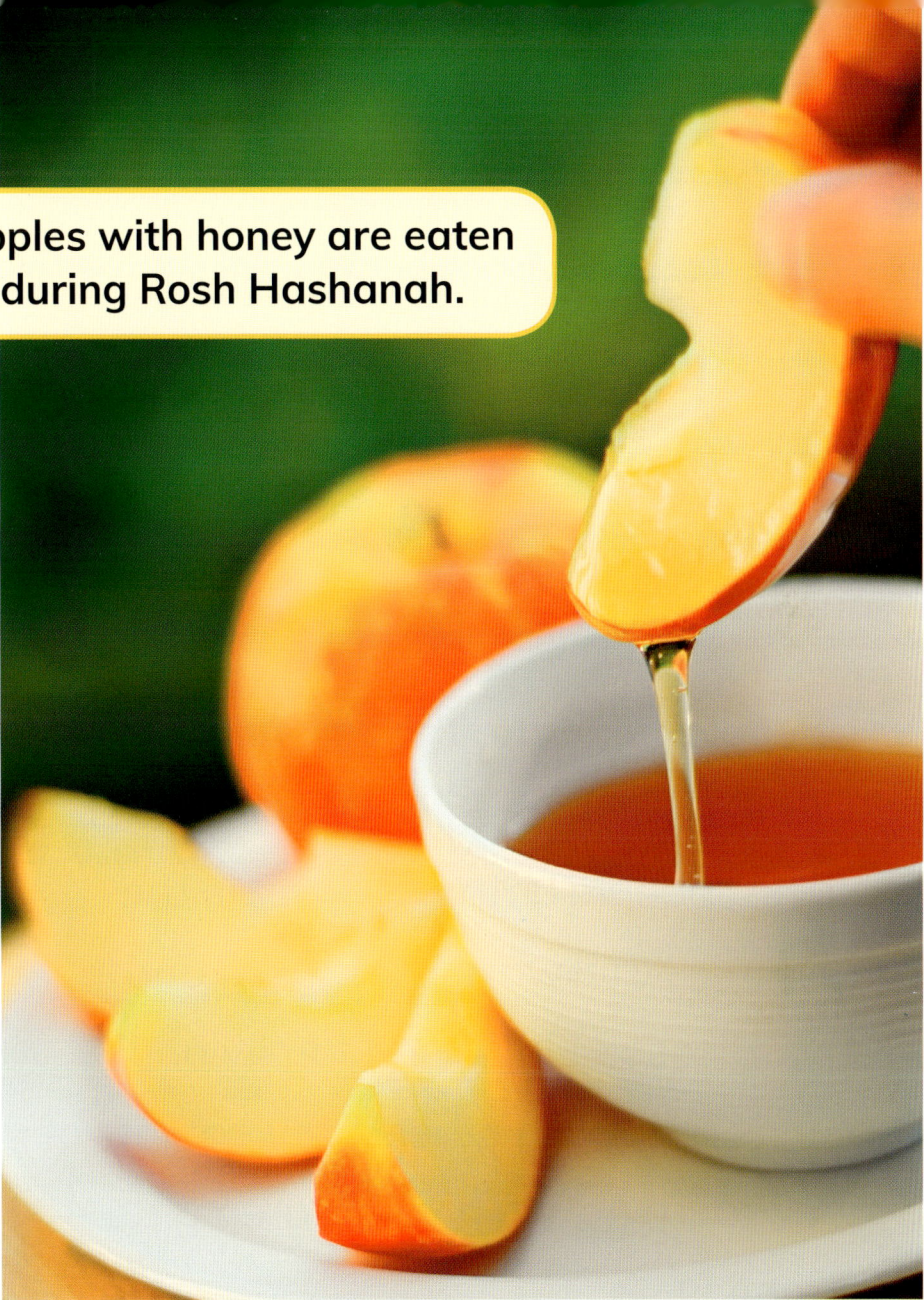

Later, many families eat apple slices dipped in honey. It means they will have a sweet year!

One month every year, **Muslims** around the world fast. They don't eat during the day. This time of fasting is called Ramadan. It's a time to pray and be kind.

People celebrate the end of fasting with Eid al-Fitr. In Pakistan and other places, people gather to pray in the morning. Afterwards, they hug and say, "Blessed Eid!" Then family and friends visit each other. They eat lots of good food. Adults give children gifts of money.

People in Pakistan say, "Blessed Eid!"

Hindus have fun during Diwali. This **festival** is usually in October or November. It lasts for five days. Diwali celebrates the power of good over evil.

Lighting lamps for Diwali

Patterns made of flowers or coloured sand are called *rangoli*.

In India, lights and oil lamps fill the streets. They light up homes too. People also make pretty patterns on the ground with flowers or coloured sand. They believe these decorations will lead a goddess into their home. She will bring happiness to the whole family.

Buddhists celebrate Buddha's birthday. It is a time to remember the life of the Buddha. It is often in May or April.

During the celebrations, many people bring food and flowers to their local **temple**. In South Korea and other places, they pour water over statues of Buddha. It's a way to show thanks for his teachings. The water also reminds people to get rid of bad actions and thoughts.

A child in South Korea pours water on a statue of Buddha.

MARKING THE NEW YEAR

One year ends and a new one begins! Millions of people around the world celebrate New Year's Day on 1 January. Fireworks go off at midnight on New Year's Eve.

People in Brazil get ready to jump over ocean waves.

In many **cultures**, people do things to bring good luck. People in Brazil often wear all white. Then they jump over seven ocean waves. They make a wish on each jump.

In Estonia, some people eat nine meals. They believe it will give them the strength of nine people in the year ahead.

Not everyone celebrates the new year on 1 January. People in Iran mark it on the same day that spring begins. This is called Nowruz. People clean their homes. They wear new clothes. It's time for a fresh start.

Many cultures in Asia look forward to the Lunar New Year. It's in January or February. Adults in China give children red envelopes with money inside. Firecrackers go off during colourful parades. *Bang!* The sound scares away evil.

A Lunar New Year parade in China

CELEBRATE YOUR COUNTRY

Are you proud of your country? Many have celebrations to mark important days in their history. In the United States, 4 July is Independence Day. It's the day the country became free. Families and friends have picnics. Parades with floats go through town.

An Independence Day parade

A Bastille Day parade

People in France celebrate their country with Bastille Day. Soldiers march in a huge parade. At night, fireworks light up the sky.

HOLIDAYS THAT HELP US REMEMBER

Many cultures have holidays to honour loved ones who have died. In Mexico, they have the Day of the Dead. People put up photos of those who are gone. They set out food and gifts for the spirits to enjoy. Many people dress up like skeletons.

Children dress up for the Day of the Dead.

Carrying lanterns to the water for the end of Obon

People in Japan have Obon. They believe spirits of dead family members visit during this festival. When it's over, people place lanterns in the river. The lights guide the spirits back.

Other days honour people who died keeping their countries safe. In Australia and New Zealand, they have Anzac Day. It remembers those who died in war. People sing, pray and read poems.

An Anzac Day event in Australia

Poppy flower wreaths made of paper

The UK has Remembrance Day. People wear poppies and place them on the graves of soldiers. Everyone is silent for two minutes at 11 am. This shows respect for soldiers who have given their lives.

HARVEST TIME

Are you thankful for food? Some people celebrate the **harvest**. In West Africa, there are many different yam festivals. In Ghana, a leader prays for the yams to grow. Then he takes a bite of one. Now everybody eats yams! People play music and dance.

A leader prays during a yam festival in Ghana.

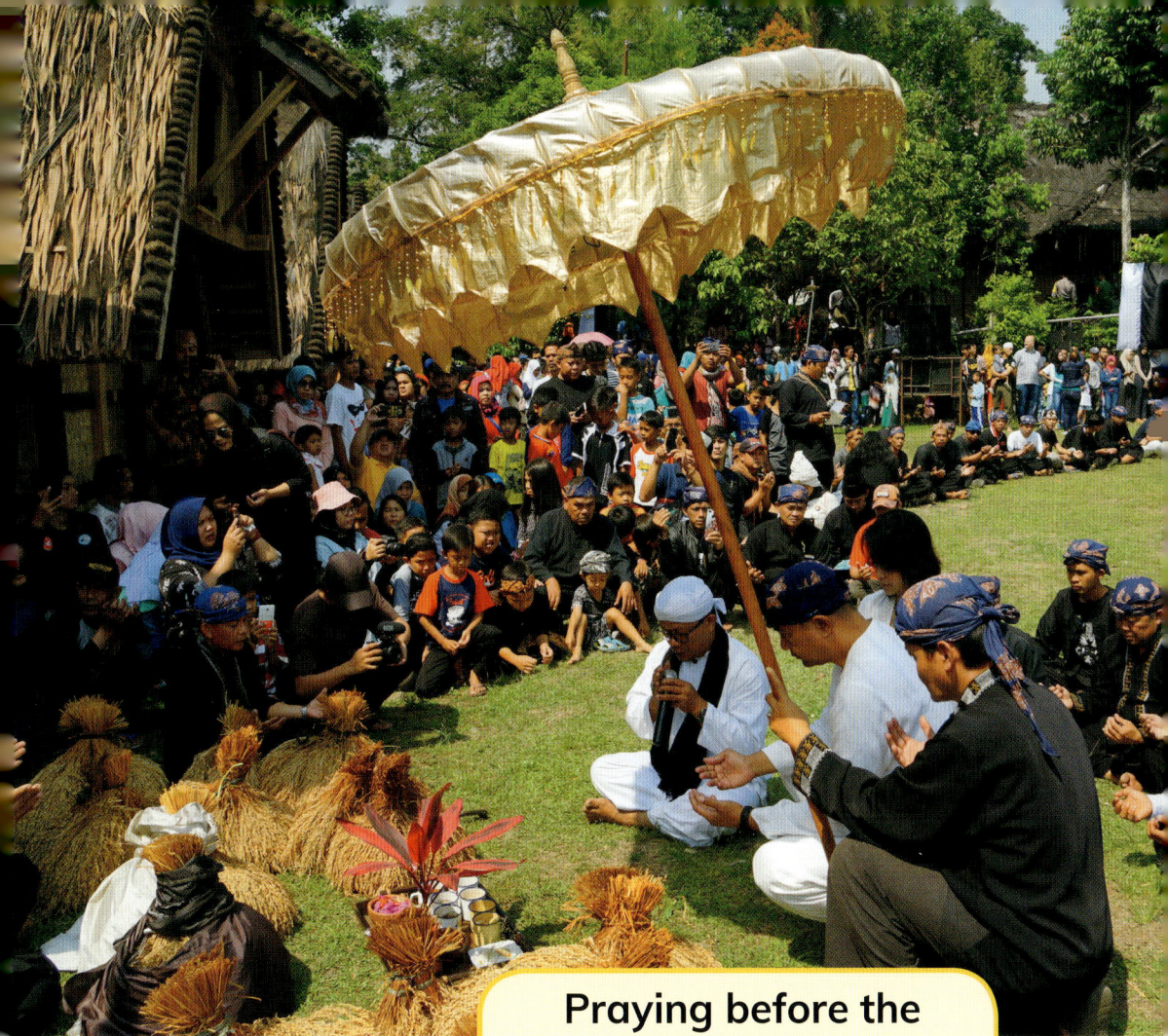

Praying before the picked rice is put away

The rice harvest is a festival time in Indonesia. Before farmers put the rice away, people pray. They thank the rice goddess for a good harvest. They eat special rice dishes.

It doesn't matter where someone lives. It doesn't matter what religion they follow. There are many special things in life that we can all come together to celebrate.

What celebration is next on your calendar? What will you do to make it special?

MAP

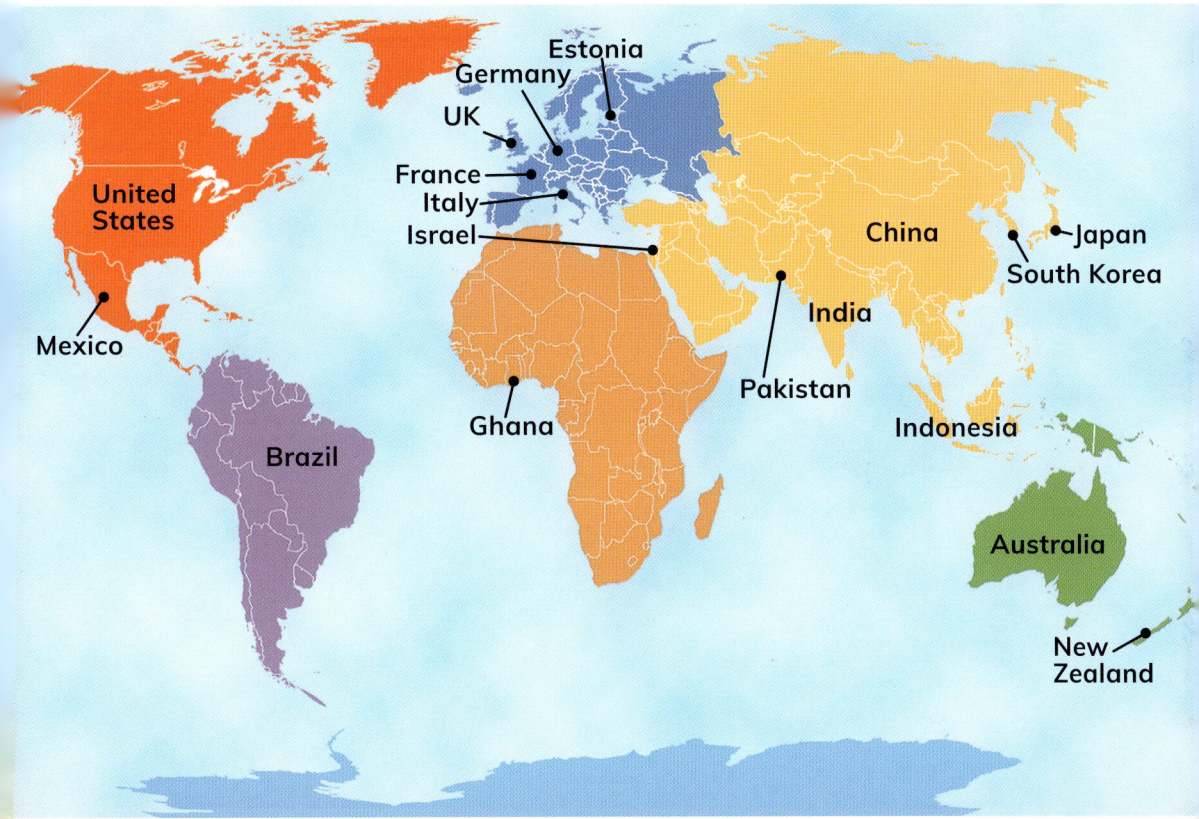

Estonia
Germany
UK
France
Italy
Israel
United States
Mexico
Brazil
Ghana
China
Japan
South Korea
India
Pakistan
Indonesia
Australia
New Zealand

Around the world, people celebrate different things. See which places were talked about in this book!

GLOSSARY

Buddhist person who follows Buddhism, a religion based on the teachings of Buddha

celebrate do something for a special event

Christian person who follows Christianity, a religion based on the teachings of Jesus

culture group of people's way of life

custom usual way of doing something in a place or for a group of people

decoration pretty, shiny or colourful thing used to make something look nice

festival time with special activities

harvest time when farmers pick and gather all the food they have grown

Hindu person who follows Hinduism, a religion that looks for truths about the meaning of life

Jewish relating to Judaism, a religion based on belief in God and the holy book called the Torah

Muslim person who follows Islam, a religion based on belief in one god called Allah and that Muhammad is his prophet

temple building used for worship

FIND OUT MORE

BOOKS

Celebrating Buddhist Festivals (Celebration Days), Nick Hunter (Raintree, 2016)

Celebrations Around the World: The Fabulous Celebrations You Won't Want to Miss, Katy Halford (DK Children, 2019)

Children Just Like Me: A New Celebration of Children Around the World, DK (DK Children, 2016)

WEBSITES

www.bbc.co.uk/bitesize/topics/z478gwx/articles/zb33pg8
Learn more about different celebrations.

www.dkfindout.com/uk/more-find-out/festivals-and-holidays
Find out more about festivals and holidays around the world.

INDEX